AF606679

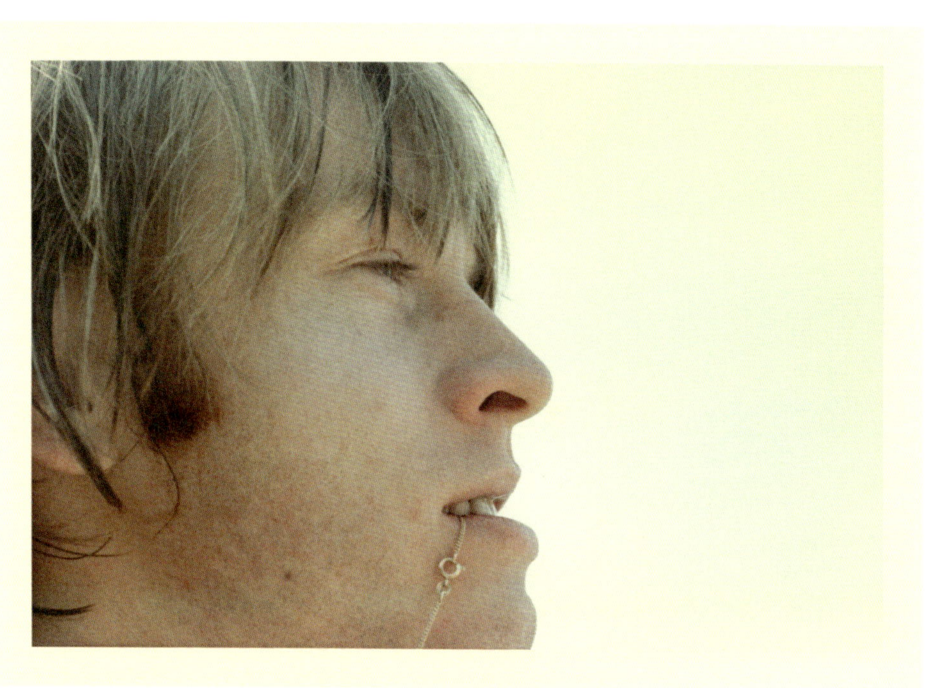

Found: The Rolling Stones

All photographs from the collection of Lauren White
Edited by Lauren White and George Augusto

Design: Michael Schmelling / 40 Worth St.
Coördination: Jacques Marlow, Michael Shifflet

The photographs reproduced here were found and purchased at a public flea market in Southern California in 2012. The dates and locations of the pictures can be deduced in some detail from the content of the images, but, despite numerous attempts to determine the provenance of the prints, at the time of this publication the photographer remains unknown.

http:/foundrollingstones.com

ISBN: 978-0-9897859-2-1
Printed by Optimal Media

Distributed in North America by Artbook/DAP
http://artbook.com

THE ICE PLANT • LOS ANGELES

Found:
The Rolling Stones

Edited by

Lauren White and George Augusto

Essay by

John Jeremiah Sullivan

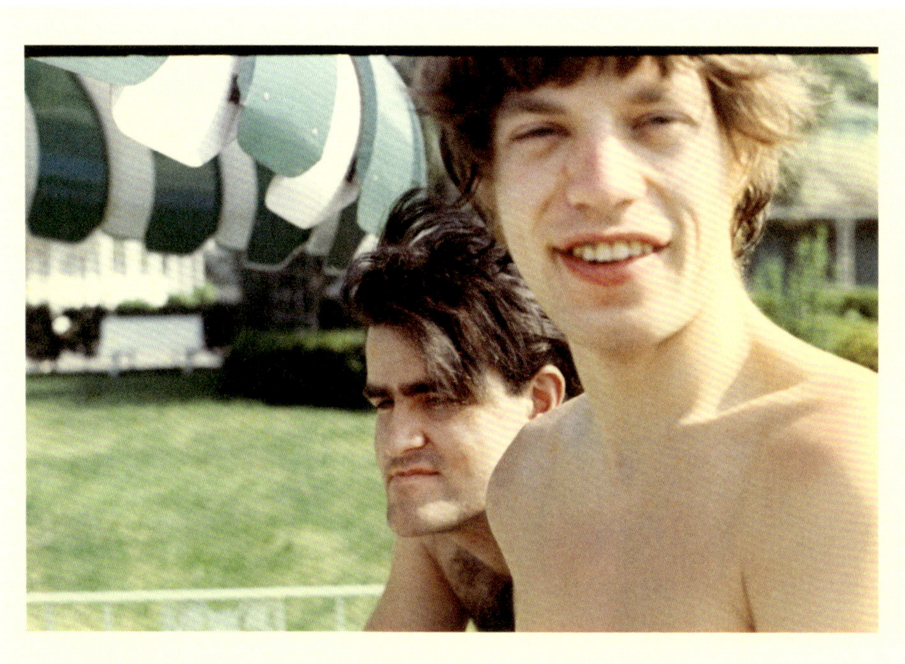

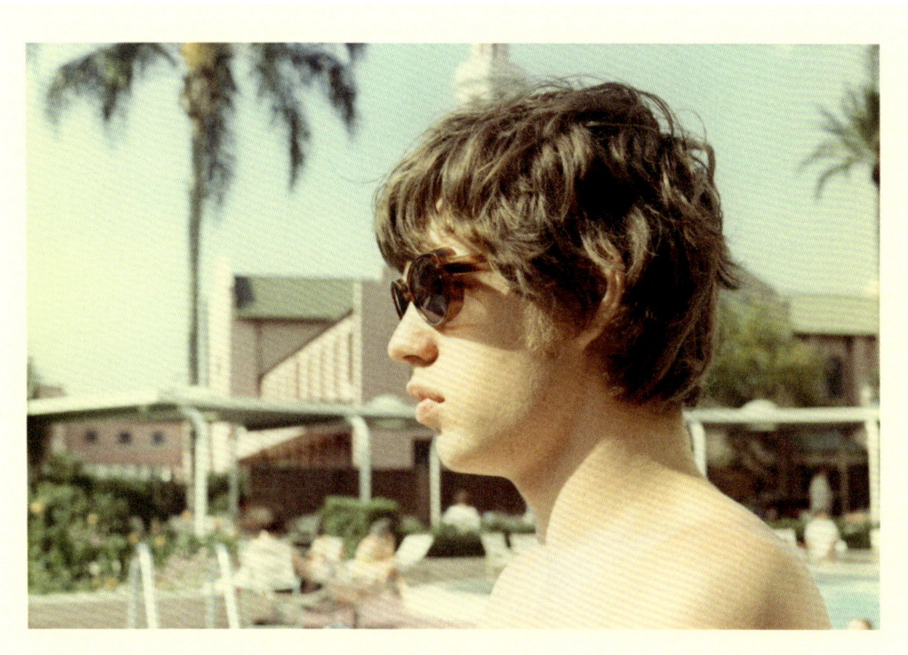

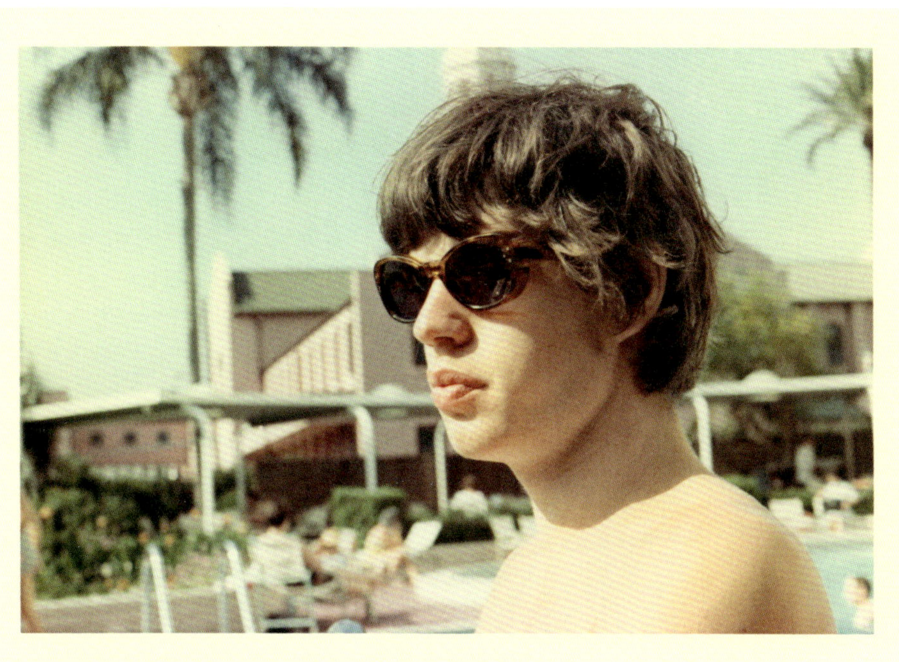

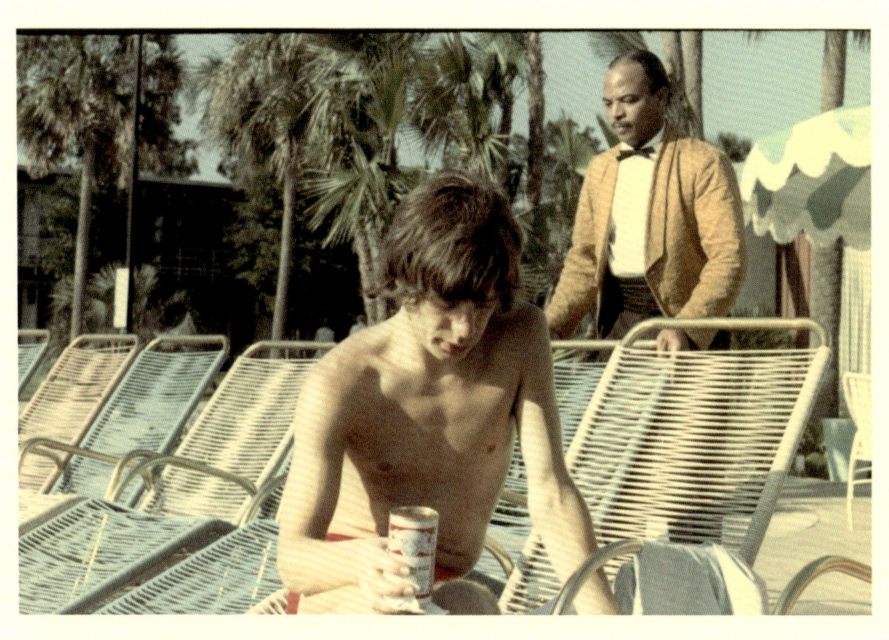

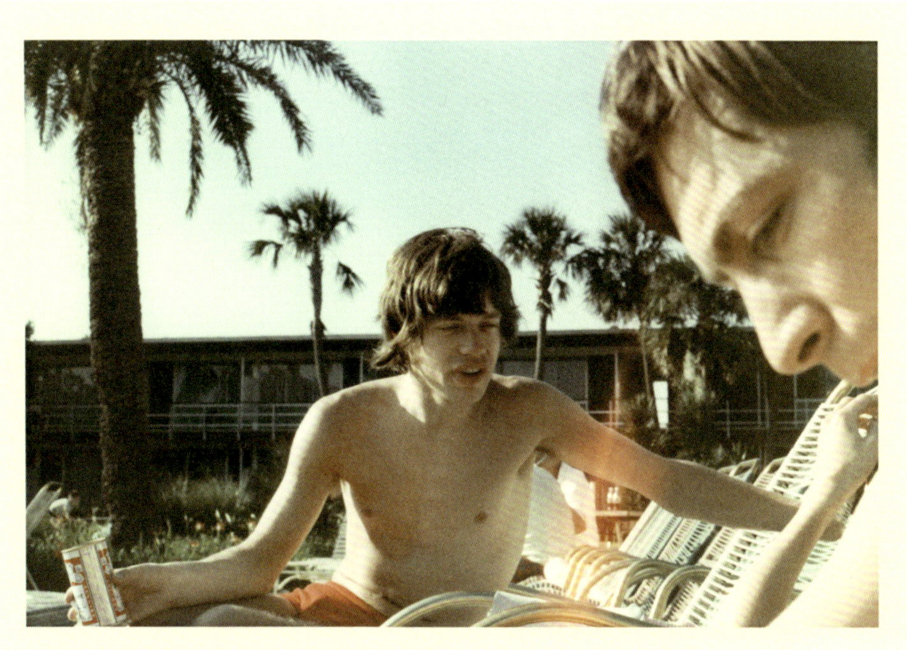

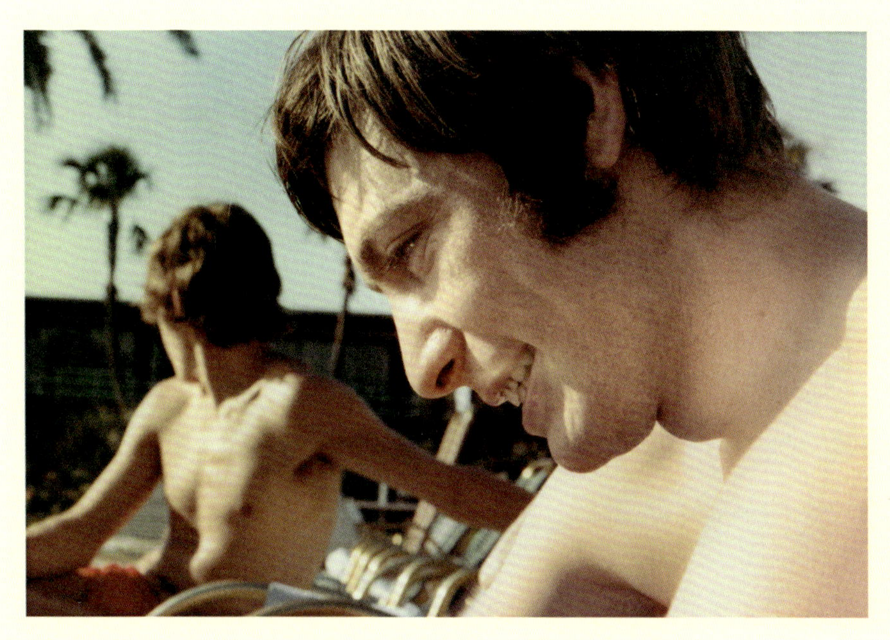

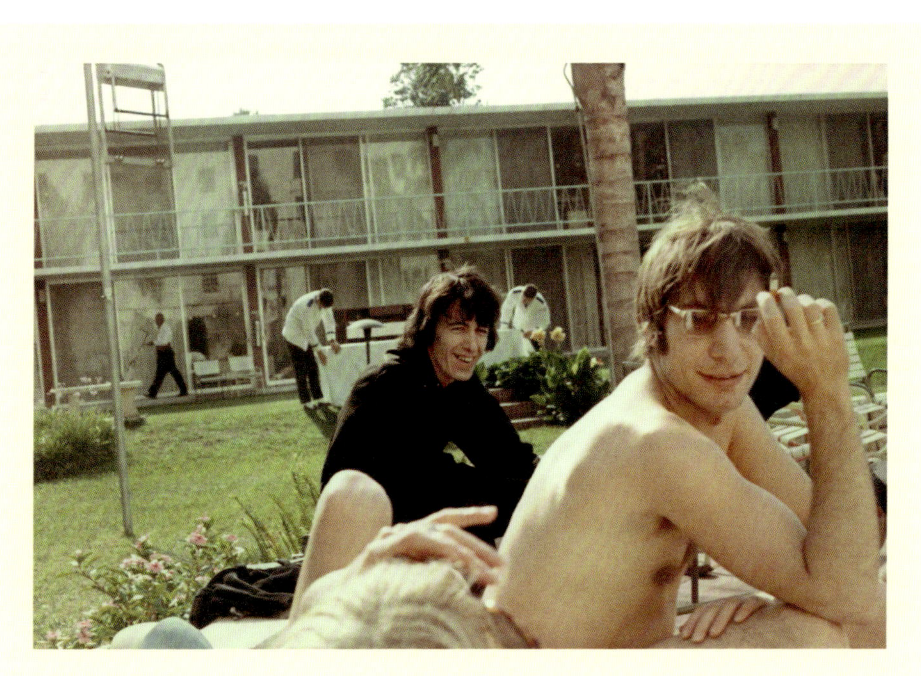

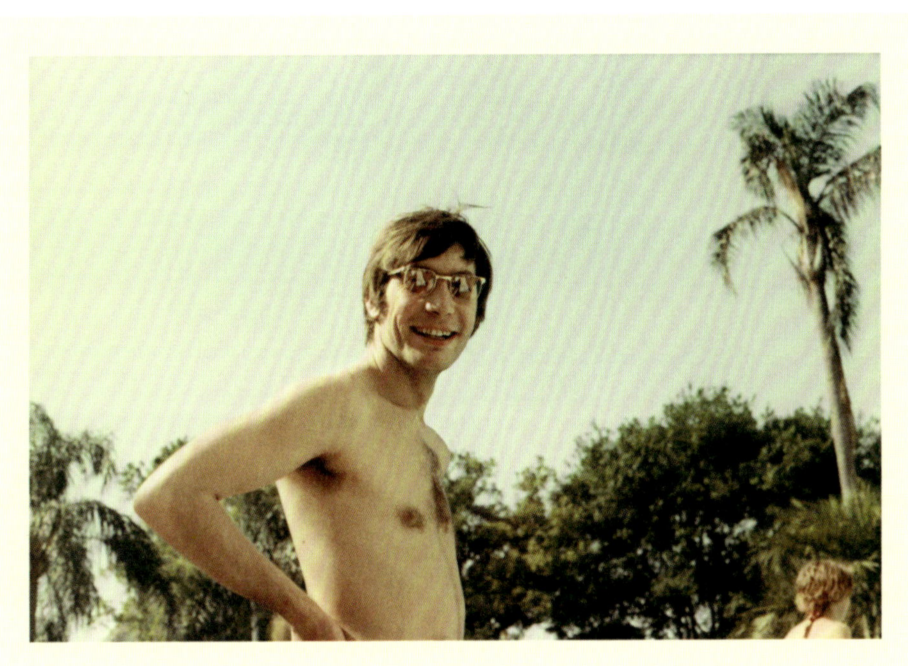

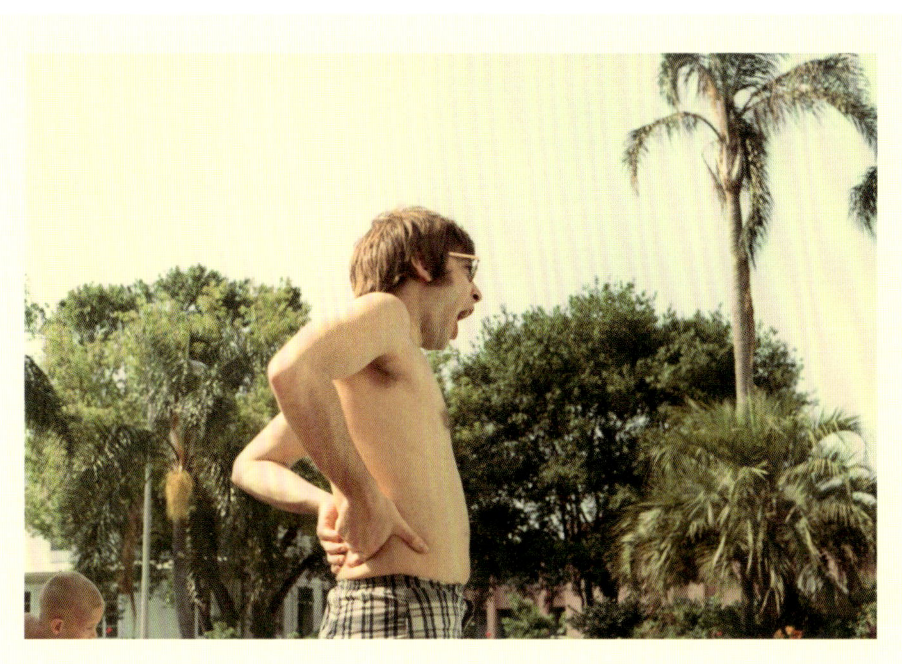

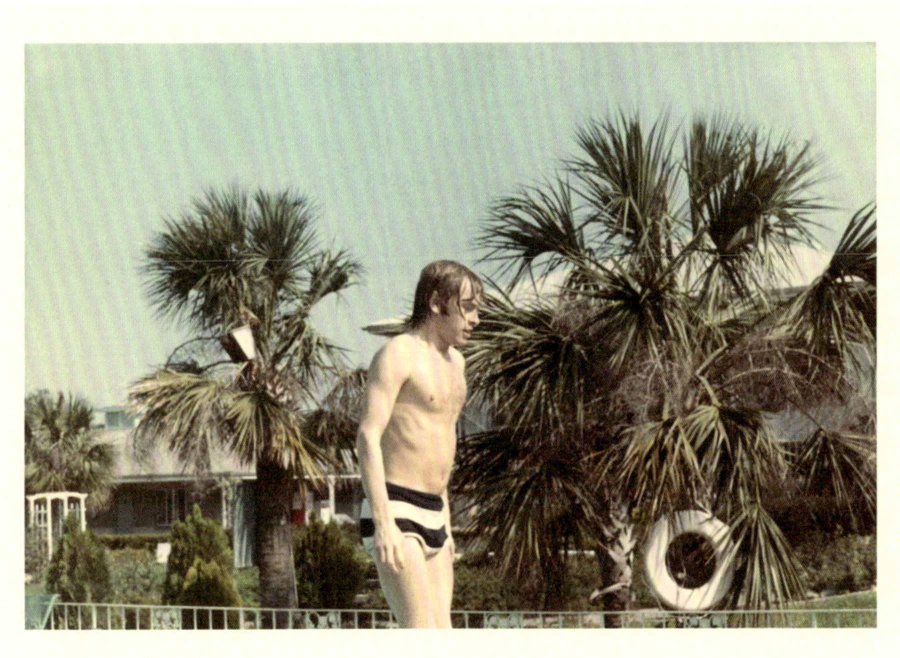

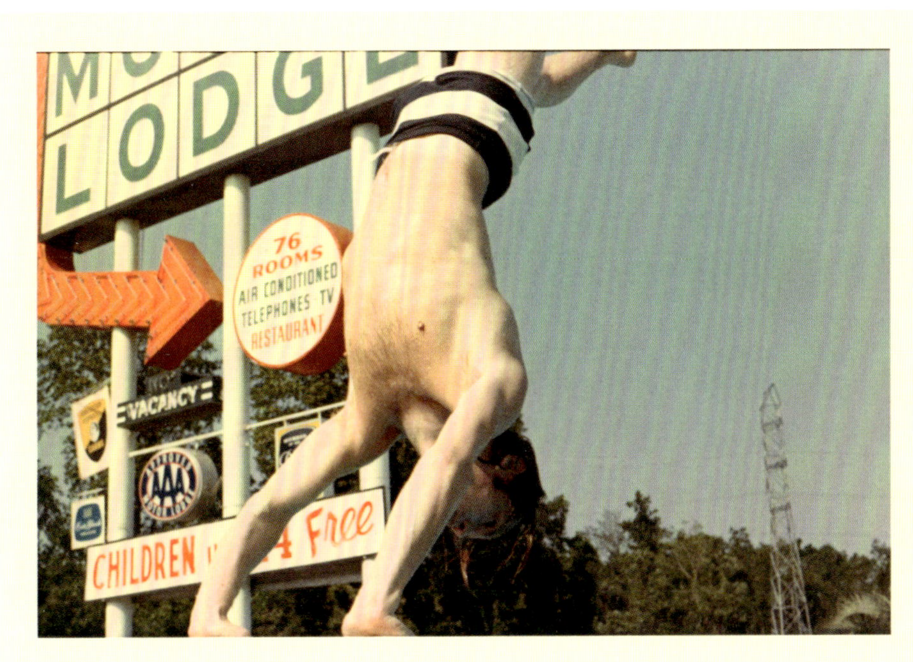
LODGE
76
ROOMS
AIR CONDITIONED
TELEPHONES TV
RESTAURANT
VACANCY
AAA
CHILDREN
Free

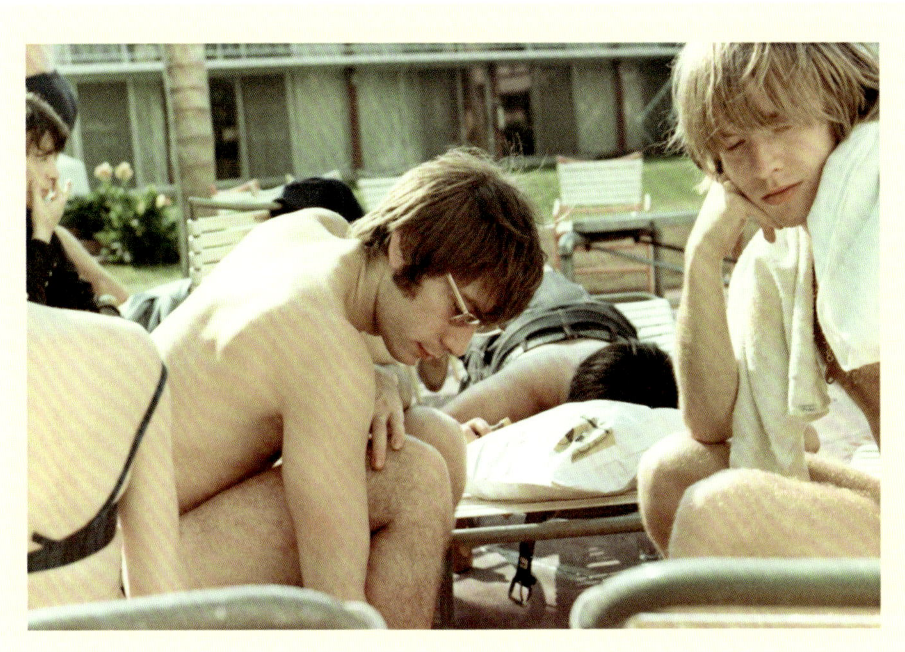

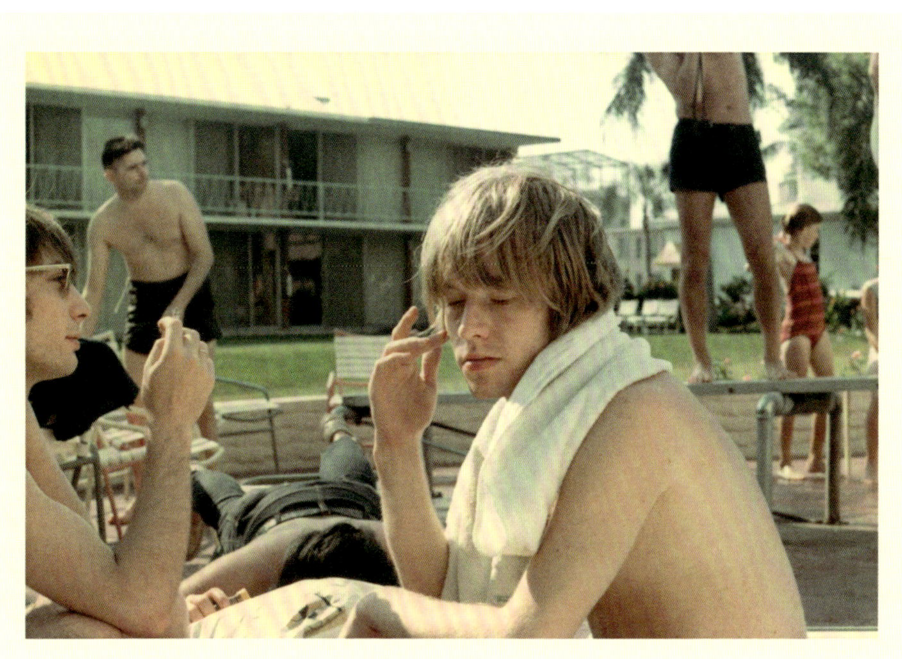

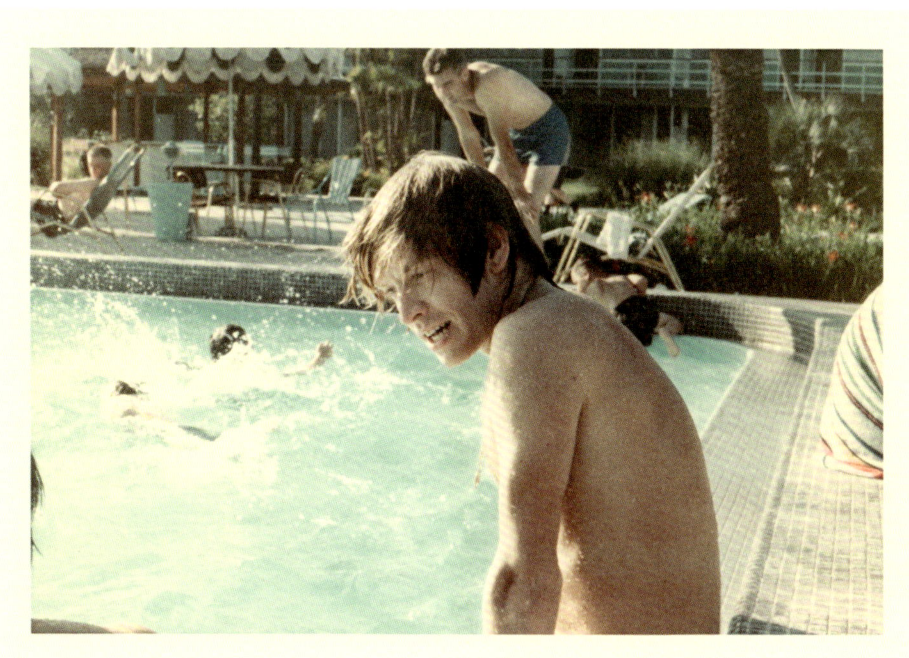

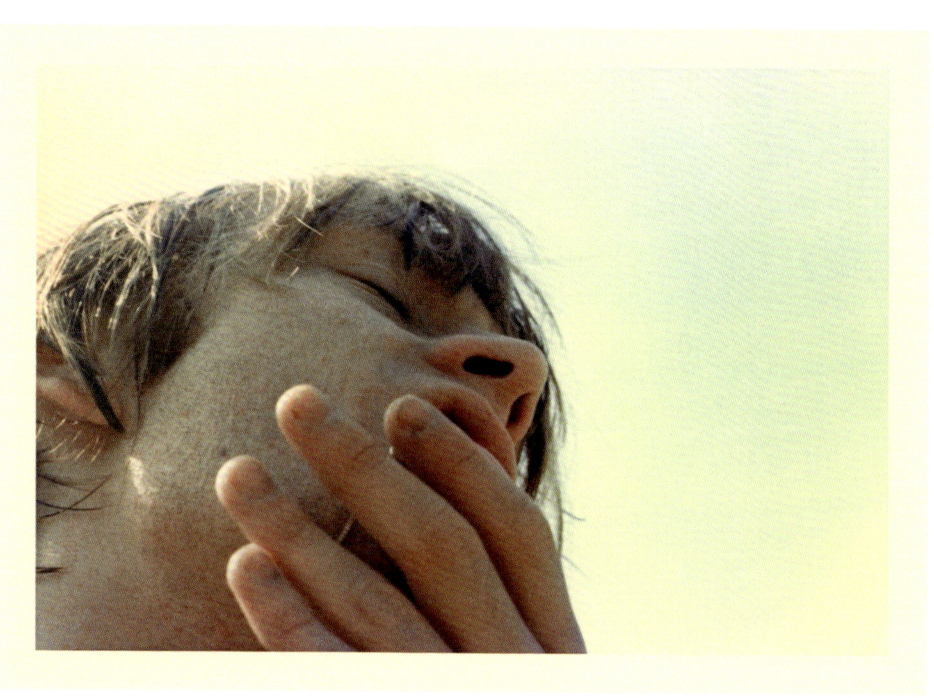

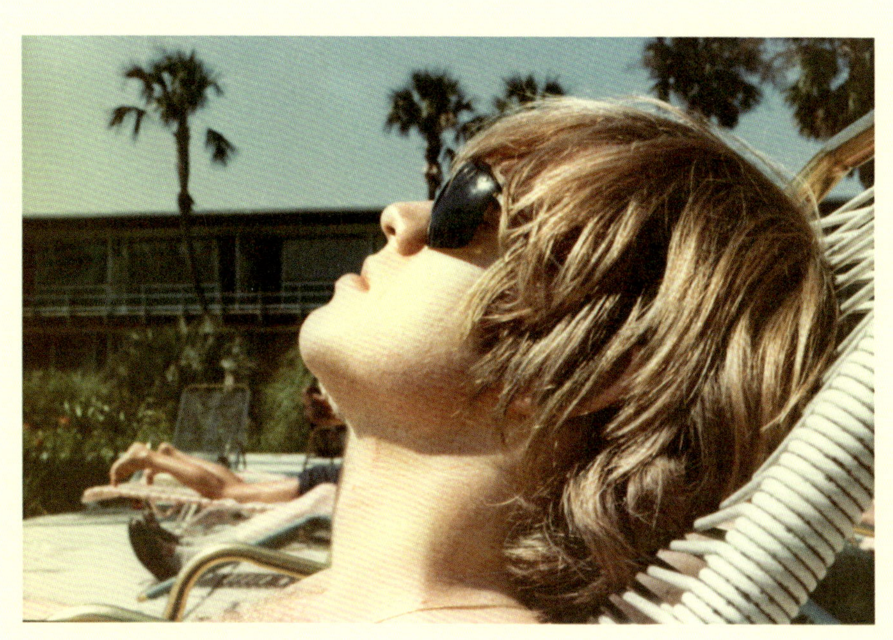

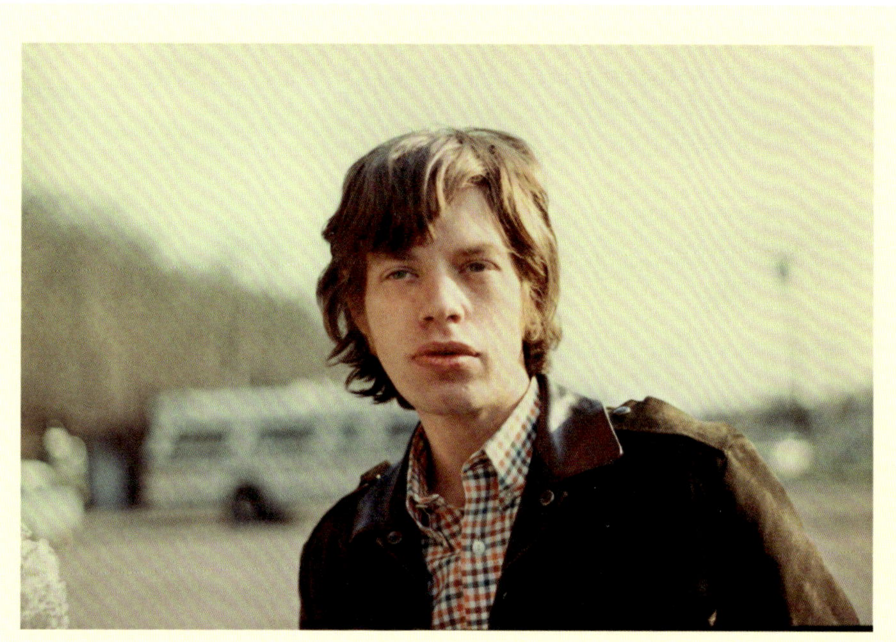

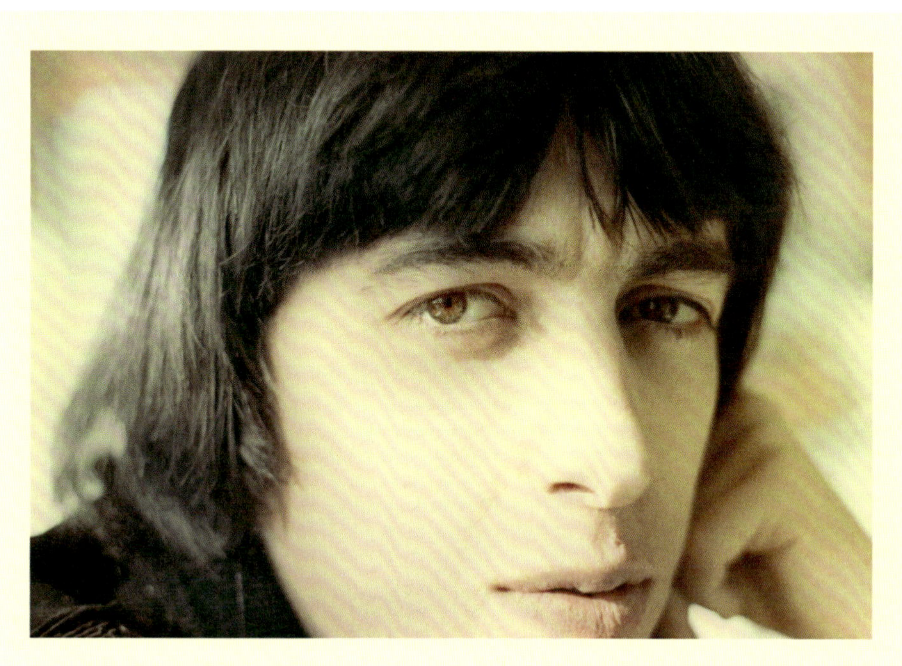

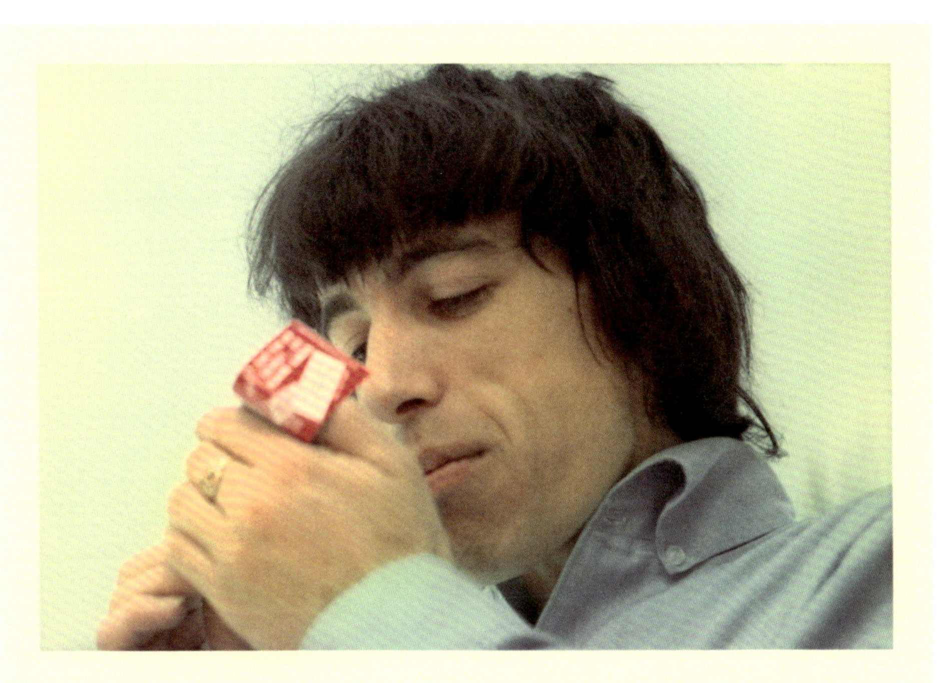

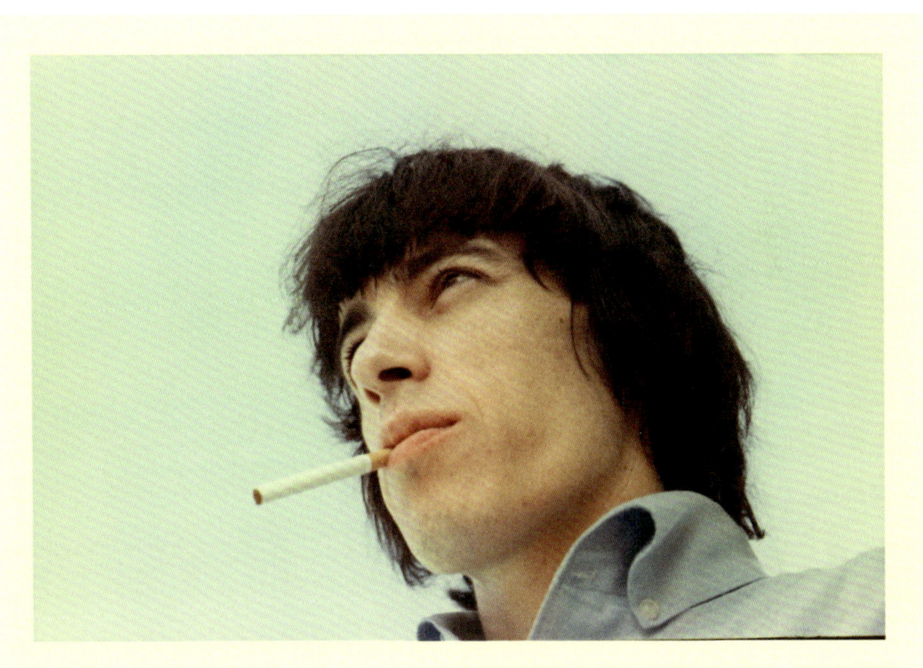

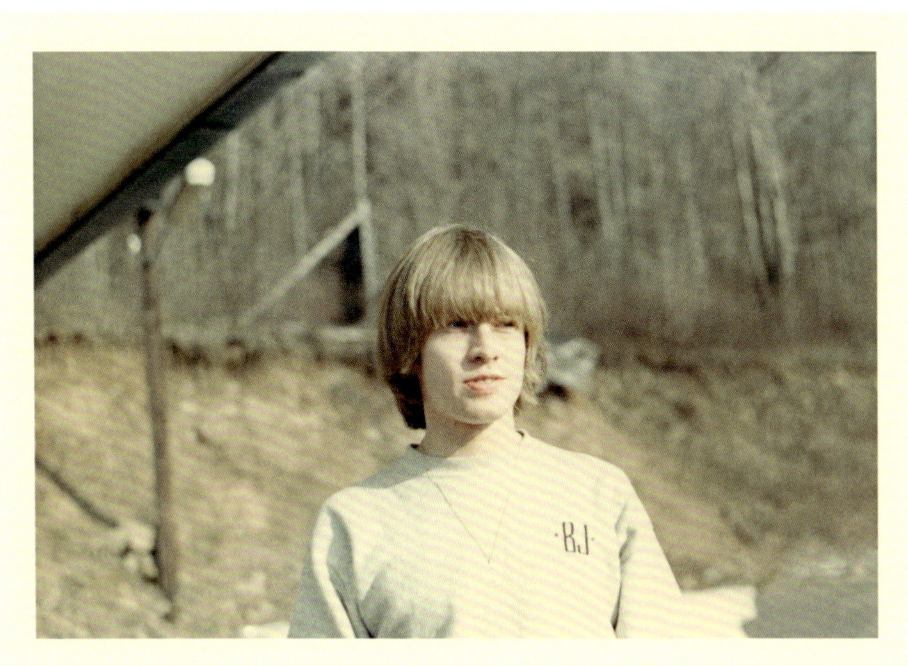
·B.J·

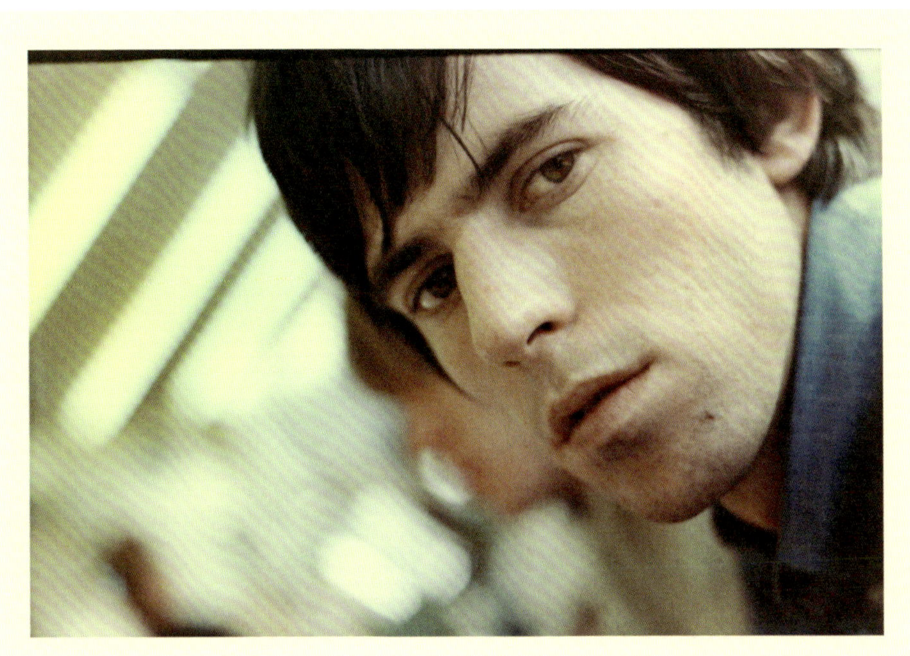

The photographs in this book were found by Lauren White in 2012, and exhibited at Dilettante gallery in Los Angeles shortly thereafter. As of this publication, the identity of photographer remains unknown. We sent the pictures to The Paris Review's *Southern Editor, John Jeremiah Sullivan, for comment and speculation.*

Jacques Marlow, The Ice Plant, July 2014

Dear Mr. Marlow,

Thanks for letting me see the photographs. There's definitely something spookily pre-Altamont Apocalypse about them. A 22-year-old Brian Jones flipping playfully into the pool like a shining blonde champion of the dawn... How does one "comment" on that! Hard to believe they were found at a flea market, just insofar as I can't believe they got passed around for fifty years without anyone's realizing what they were. Must have come straight from an estate sale. But they were taken mostly in the south, and you say they turned up somewhere in California. Confusing. Eventually someone will figure out who the photographer is and we'll have no choice but to look at them in a certain way, since the eye of the photographer is so important to us and even a little tyrannical, when you think about it. I like not knowing. For about four seconds. Could they be snapshots taken by Bob Bonis, the Stones' road manager on that tour in 1965, their second American tour? He was a respected amateur photographer and did shoot them a lot during that period, in fact on some of the same days, in Georgia and Florida. So did a couple of college boys from North Carolina—Kevin Delaney and Steve Denenberg—who'd hitchhiked down to see the Stones play and took backstage Instamatic pictures of the band members. But in neither case do the other pictures quite seem to match up. Further obscuring matters, a cropped version of one of the shots appeared in an issue of *Tiger Beat* magazine in 1966, identified as having been taken in Hollywood, and with no photographer named. Multiple anonymous Internet sleuths are to thank for those details, which leave us no less in the dark.

I kept going back to the cluster of shots that mainly show Mick and Charlie Watts wearing shades and sitting in those plastic chaise chairs, by the pool. If I'm not mistaken we think it's at the Fort Harrison Hotel in Clearwater, Florida, the day after their Clearwater show. At first I grew fixated on them because I'd become convinced that a reflection of the photographer might be preserved in the lenses of their dark glasses, a tiny image that could then be blown up using advanced technology. But evidently there isn't enough to work with. The grain in the originals wasn't fine enough. We can see a smudge there that we know is him or her with the camera but no more.

In staring at those particular pictures so much, I noticed that there appears to be a young woman in a few of them. In one, on page 13, the one where Mick is holding a beer can in his hand and talking to someone, her, you can see her wrist in the bottom right corner. Then in the shot on page 17, that also has a smiling Bill Wyman in the background, you can see her straw-blonde hair, and the curve of her knee, and a few of her fingers as she holds up her hand to shade her eyes from the sun. Charlie is smoking and smiling at her. In another picture, on page 27, you can see her shoulder blade and back, and the strap of her bra or bikini top, which is sliding off, down her arm. Finally that may be her again in one of the later pictures, from London, toward the end of the book, the one in which Keith is sitting there looking magnificently stoned, and you see a girl's short blonde haircut swishing against the side of her face as she spins in a blue jacket.

People have written that these pictures come from a time when the Stones were "on the brink of mega-stardom," but does everyone realize how uncannily precise that is? If we can believe Keith Richards (who else are we meant to believe?), these pictures—the ones from Florida—were taken not only on the very day but during the very moments in which Mick wrote the lyrics to "(I Can't Get No) Satisfaction," the song that would change everything for the band, take them from being "another mop-haired, British singing group," as the Florida papers described them, to one that might contest The Beatles' throne. "Mick wrote the lyrics by the pool in Clearwater, Florida," Richards writes in *Life*, his memoir. The Stones spent only twenty-four hours in town on that tour. Arrived in the evening, played a show at a ballpark, and left the next afternoon. So there are just a few hours—between, say, 11:00am and 2:00pm, on May 7th—that Keith could be remembering when he writes "by the pool in Clearwater."

The show the night before, in Jack Russell Stadium, had been a somewhat hilarious bust. It started at 7:00pm. Opening acts were The Roemans (a Florida garage band), The Legends (Milwaukee rock), The Catalinas (beach music from Charlotte), and The Intruders (Philly soul). But when The Stones took the stage, the teenage fans rioted, overwhelming a barrier and a line of police. A somewhat scary picture of a few fans appeared later in the *St. Petersburg Times*.

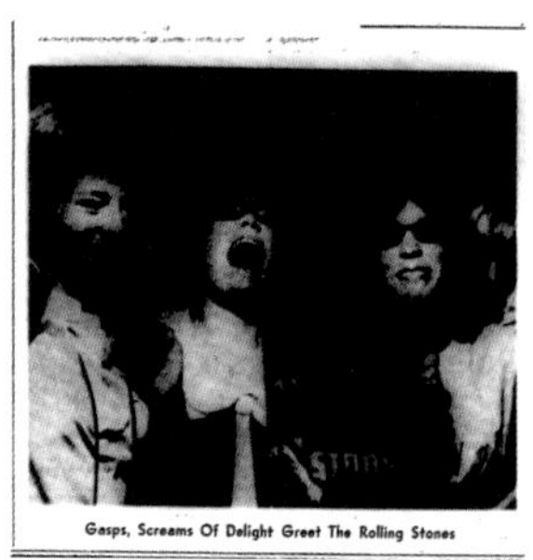

Gasps, Screams Of Delight Greet The Rolling Stones

The band was hustled into a white station wagon and driven from the field. "There will never be another show like this as long as I am here," said the head of Clearwater's recreation department, Gary Garretson.

It's the next day, by the pool. Mick's drinking a Budweiser that has been brought to him by a middle-aged black man in a white tuxedo. You can see the man in one of the pictures. Serving drinks to this unintelligible fruitcake. Mick has words running through his head. "And I'm trying to make some girl... " Who is she?

A couple of hours later and the band is again being hustled toward a waiting car. Out of the hotel, this time, and into the garage. A local reporter jogs along down the hallways, a woman from Tarpon Springs named Frances Brush.

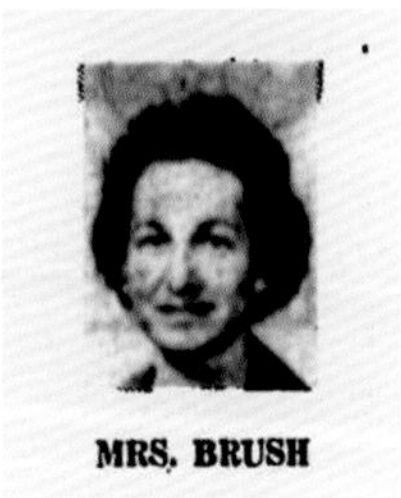
MRS. BRUSH

According to Brush, "large groups of boys and girls" had "converged" on the hotel and "entered every available entrance in their efforts to get to the musical stars." But police and "hotel officials" had succeeded in keeping them away.

"Only one girl," Brush writes, had been able to "get to the 'rock men,'" and this girl was there to say goodbye when they left. Could it be the one from the pool? Brush describes her as an 18-year-old "pretty blonde," an English girl living in the States, who'd known "the boys" back in London. Her name was Ginny French. She'd been hanging out with them. Seems like it has to be her. If "Satisfaction" has a muse, she is Ginny French.

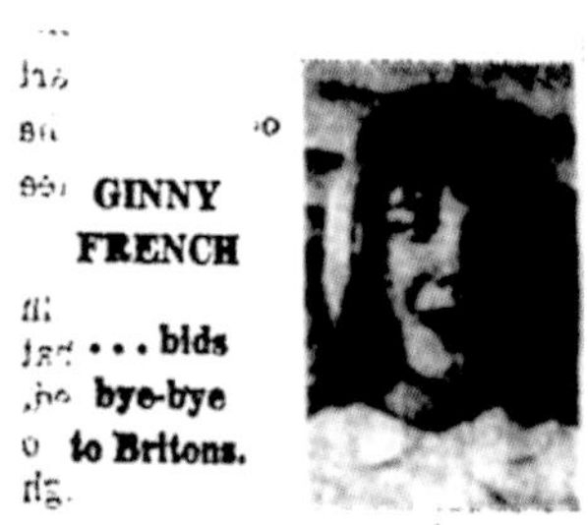
GINNY FRENCH
. . . bids bye-bye to Britons.

Brush asks Ginny about the non-show from the night before, if the Stones had been frightened at all. "Ginny said the boys were not particularly disturbed by the incident that disrupted their show since 'this sort of thing happens all the time.'"

I couldn't find anything else about a girl named Ginny French and The Rolling Stones. Who knows how much longer French was even her name. Presumably she's out there.

Before the band took off, Mrs. Brush asked Brian Jones, "What do you plan to do when this bubble bursts?"

Jones smiled and said, "We'll blow another bubble."

I wish I had more.

Sincerely,

John S.

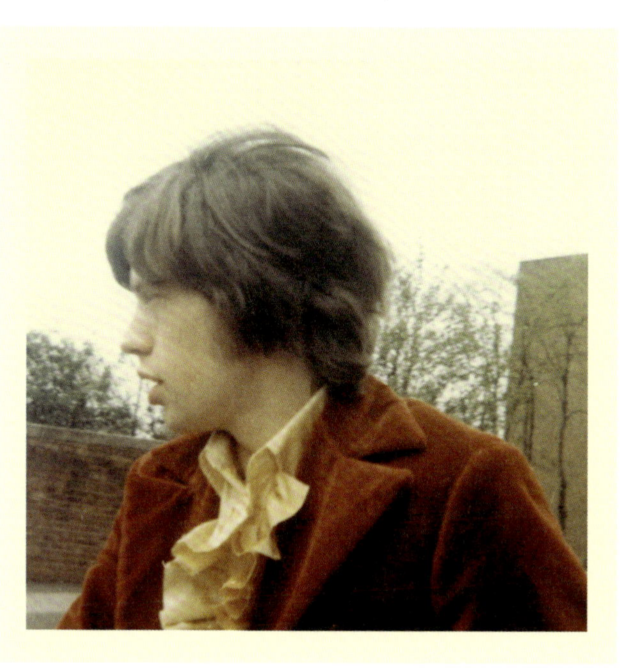

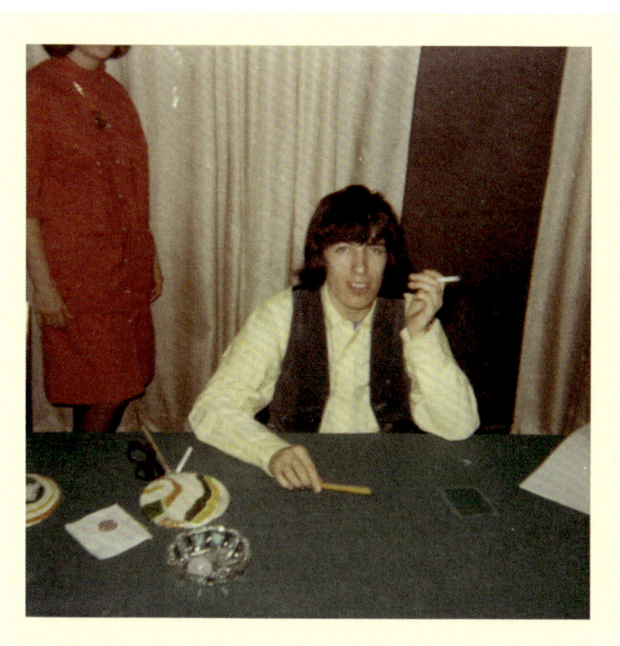

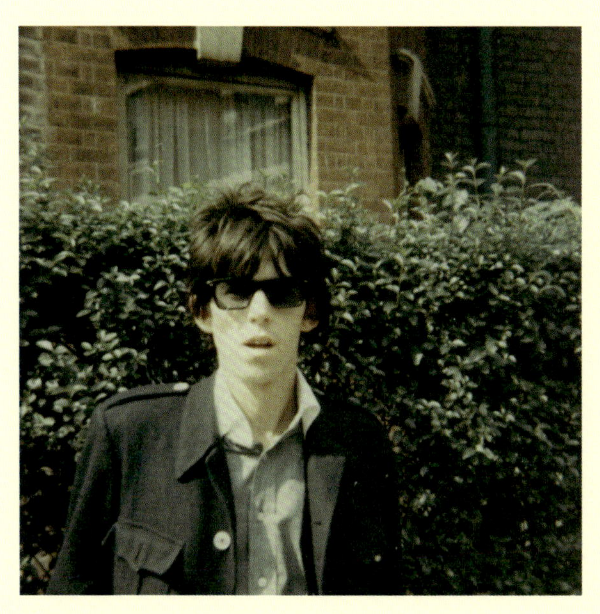

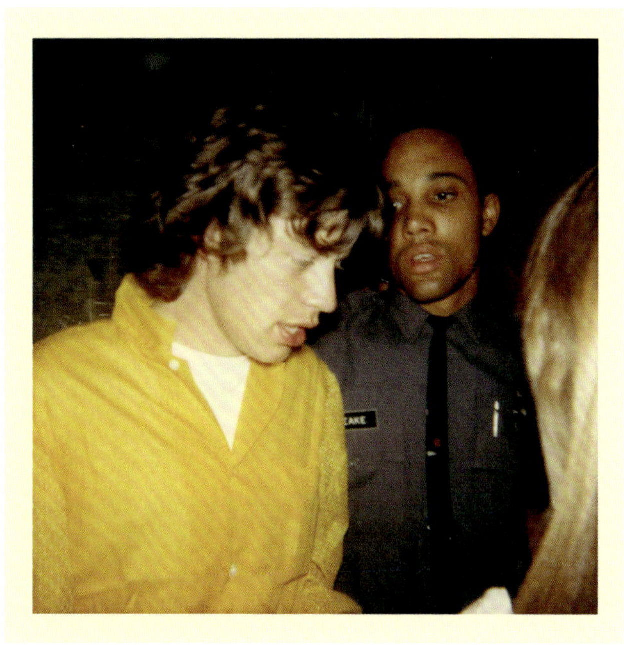

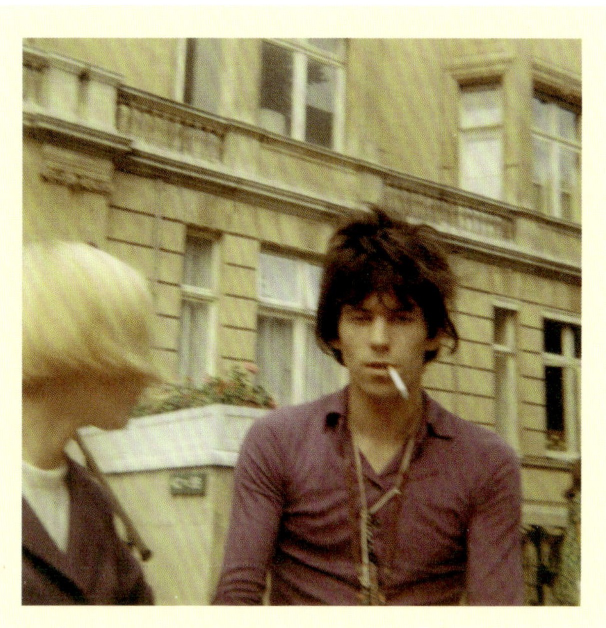

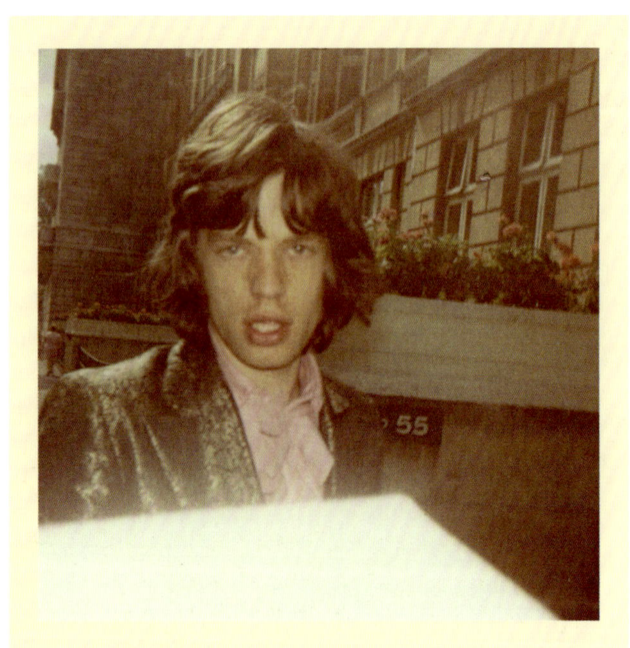
55